IT'S Me.

How do I Embrace Who I was made to be?

Participant's Guide

A Reel to Real Study

Nicole Johnson
Mary E. Demuth

THOMAS NELSON
Since 1798

NASHVILLE   DALLAS   MEXICO CITY   RIO DE JANEIRO

Published in Nashville, Tennessee, by Thomas Nelson. Thomas Nelson is a registered trademark of Thomas Nelson, Inc.

Thomas Nelson, Inc., titles may be purchased in bulk for educational, business, fund-raising, or sales promotional use. For information, please e-mail SpecialMarkets@thomasnelson.com.

All Scripture quotations, unless otherwise indicated, are taken from the HOLY BIBLE: NEW INTERNATIONAL VERSION®. Copyright © 1973, 1978, 1984 by International Bible Society. Used by permission of Zondervan Publishing House. All rights reserved.

Scripture quotations marked ESV are from THE ENGLISH STANDARD VERSION. © 2001 by Crossway Bibles, a division of Good News Publishers.

Scripture quotations marked MSG are from *The Message* by Eugene H. Peterson. © 1993, 1994, 1995, 1996, 2000. Used by permission of NavPress Publishing Group. All rights reserved.

Scripture quotations marked NASB are taken from the NEW AMERICAN STANDARD Bible®. © The Lockman Foundation 1960, 1962, 1963, 1968, 1971, 1972, 1973, 1975, 1977. Used by permission.

Scripture quotations marked NCV are taken from the New Century Version®. © 2005 by Thomas Nelson, Inc. Used by permission. All rights reserved. Scripture quotations marked NKJV are from THE NEW KING JAMES VERSION. © 1982 by Thomas Nelson, Inc. Used by permission. All rights reserved.

Scripture quotations marked NKJV are taken from THE NEW KING JAMES VERSION. © 1982 by Thomas Nelson, Inc. Used by permission. All rights reserved.

Scripture quotations marked NLT are from the *Holy Bible*, New Living Translation. © 1996. Used by permission of Tyndale House Publishers, Inc., Wheaton, Illinois 60189. All rights reserved.

Poem on page 73 is taken from *Thin Places* by Mary E. DeMuth. Copyright © 2010 by Mary E. DeMuth. Used by permission of Zondervan. www.zondervan.com.

ISBN: 978-1-4185-4628-1

Reel to Real: An Interactive Drama-Based Study Series

It's Me: How Do I Embrace Who I Was Made to Be?

Printed in the United States of America

11 12 13 14 15 QG 5 4 3 2 1

contents:

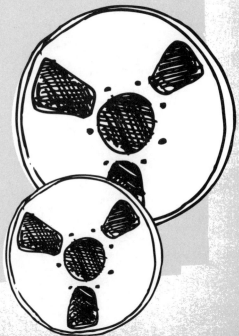

What Is a Reel to Real Study?

Simply put, it's what you hold in your hands. A video sketch (reel) and your journey (real). Put those two together and you have a fresh and transforming way of studying the Bible and getting to know God.

We are so excited you've decided to journey alongside us in this adventure called following Jesus. Knowing the current bent toward YouTube, iTunes, and social networking sites, we've developed an interactive study based on that reality. You'll watch a drama, hear from others who are on the journey, and then chat about it with your friends. We've provided many different ways for you to grow.

The sketches you'll see on the DVD are dramatic vignettes written and directed by Nicole Johnson. Each drama was performed and recorded live at the Revolve Tour and put together for this study as a creative way to look at the issues we face.

This guide will be your companion as you watch the dramas. The first study is designed for group interaction. Of course, you can always watch the DVD on your own and work your way through the study if you'd like. But we find gathering a group of friends to watch the drama, then discussing it together over popcorn and caffeine makes the learning fun. More people equal more discussion, more insight.

After the initial watch and discuss, we offer four more studies for you to explore each theme on your own. Like taking a walk in your own woods, you can go as deep as you dare and stay as long as you wish, hopefully emerging at some point with a clearer understanding of how you can live differently in this changing world.

These personal studies will not be your typical Bible study where you take a crusty ballpoint and fill in long blanks with short answers. We'll ask you probing questions that definitely don't have a set answer. You'll tap into your creativity. We'll push you (gently!) toward thinking about the world outside your front door. We'll start you with a truth, but you'll end with a dare. Then we'll resource you with cool sites, books, and songs that can help you further your journey.

It's our hope that by watching this DVD, digesting it with friends, and doing some thinking and wrestling on your own, you'll finish the study a little different from how you were when you started. More confident of who you are. More able to open your heart to who God is and willing to be surprised by His extravagant, countercultural love. Released to be who He created you to be. And full of gratitude for all He has done (and will continue do) inside you and through you.

The world needs your heart. Your real heart. Not some phony replica of what you think your heart should look like—a real, unique heart. Our desire is to see that heart challenged, shaped, and doing revolutions around Jesus, as He revolves around this world.

- Nicole and Mary

P.S. For more information about the Revolve Tour or just to see what this dynamic conference is all about, check out **www.revolvetour.com**.

Introduction:

No matter where you are in life, you may struggle with issues of identity. You may ask: Who am I in relation to this big, wide world? What is my role to play? My contribution to make? Deeper still: How do I live life as a loved person? Am I really loved? How do I know?

In the context of your relationships, how do you react? Are you one person with friends, another with parents, still a different person around teachers? What about all by yourself when you turn out the light at night? What does it mean to be authentic? To be wholly, genuinely, you?

This study will help you grapple with these questions. It may even raise different questions. But most of all, it will help you think—about yourself, your motives, your deepest passions. It could bother you. Sometimes you may see parts of yourself you'd rather hide. But take courage; healing takes place when we live authentically, daring to tell the truth about ourselves.

In Psalm 51:6 (MSG), King David wrote, "What you're after is truth from the inside out."

When Jesus walked the earth, He embodied this kind of truth in the way He lived. The Bible says He was Truth personified. He lived it from the inside out. He made religious people angry. He welcomed weeping, broken women. He stooped to scoop up a child in His arms. He rescued those who felt overlooked, outcast.

Because Jesus was genuinely Himself, He gave us all the power to be completely ourselves. No masks. No lies. No saying one thing and doing another. No running around trying to please everyone on the exhausting treadmill of people-pleasing.

> *Take courage; healing takes place when we live authentically, daring to tell the truth about ourselves.*

Ultimately, who we are depends on who God is in us. Which is why we're thankful for verses like Romans 8:38–39 (NLT): "And I am convinced that nothing can ever separate us from God's love. Neither death nor life, neither angels nor demons, neither our fears for today nor our worries about tomorrow—not even the powers of hell can separate us from God's love. No power in the sky above or in the earth below—indeed, nothing in all creation will ever be able to separate us from the love of God that is revealed in Christ Jesus our Lord."

No matter who you are today on the inside—full of heartaches, joys, fears, complexities, perplexities, worries, triumphs, and conundrums—you are wildly and passionately loved by the One who made you. Sometimes the most complicated problems are solved with simple reassurances like:

Jesus loves me; this I know.
For the Bible tells me so.
Little ones to Him belong.
They are weak, but He is strong.

You may feel weak today. You may struggle with who you are, who you want to be, and the chasm that seems to exist between those two. But your weakness in this moment is a stage for Jesus to demonstrate His grace and strength. In 2 Corinthians 12:9 (MSG), Paul wrote, "And then he told me, My grace is enough; it's all you need. My strength comes into its own in your weakness. Once I heard that, I was glad to let it happen. I quit focusing on the handicap and began appreciating the gift. It was a case of Christ's strength moving in on my weakness."

Is it possible for you to begin to appreciate who you are? You're uniquely you, a forever stamp of your personality on this earth.

> Your weakness in this moment is a stage for Jesus to demonstrate His grace and strength.

And has anyone ever told you *why* you are? You are here because you are loved. "Don't be afraid . . . for you are deeply loved by God. Be at peace; take heart and be strong!" (Daniel 10:19, NLT).

That kind of peace comes from a deeper understanding of who you are and why your ME is so valuable. Our hope is that you will find that kind of peace through the questions and activities in this study. That by the end you'll embrace your unique heart. That the ME who emerges on the other side will be strong, alive, and present.

As Jim Elliot, the mid-century martyr, wrote, "Wherever you are—be all there."[1]

---

1 Elisabeth Elliot, *The Journals of Jim Elliot* (Grand Rapids: Revell, 2002).

inside out

BRIEF OUTTAKE: Kellie, Brian, Josh, and Mandy discover what it's like to be forced to tell the truth in every situation. Every time a bell rings, they must share what's really on their minds—sometimes embarrassing things. This sketch explores what it means to be okay with yourself, to risk telling the truth with others.

 watch dvd episode 1.

 GROUP STUDY:

x Truth. ⟵

Go around your circle and share the answer to these questions (and remember to tell the truth!):

Q: When was the last time you were too embarrassed to tell the truth about yourself? What happened?

Q: What do you think would've happened if you told the truth?

Q: Do you regret what you said today? Why or why not?

9

Read catherine's story:

Growing up, I saw my mom live a life that showed how important it was to always fit in. I'd watch her say one thing to a neighbor, then say another to a friend—all to be liked by everyone.

Well, somehow that rubbed off on me. Now I find myself concocting all sorts of stories that aren't true. Stupid stuff, really. Not important lies about covering up cheating or stealing. Just everyday lies.

> **I find myself concocting all sorts of stories that aren't true. Stupid stuff, really. Not important lies about covering up cheating or stealing. Just everyday lies.**

Like today. Sarah asks me if I liked the latest slasher movie. I nod my head, even though those kinds of movies creep me out. Then Jayne pulls me aside and trashes the movie, telling me how scary it was. I tell her I hate those movies. Which is the truth?

It's getting to the point that I am wondering who in the world I really am. Why do I tell lies to fit in? What would happen if I just answered honestly? I write these things down in my journal, telling myself to be authentic and all, but once I get to school, I shift into "please everyone" mode. I'm tired. So, so tired.

Q: Have you ever felt like Catherine? Tell your own story of saying one thing to please a friend when you really disagreed with your own words.

_____

_____

_____

_____

_____

_____

Word.

What does the Bible say about telling the truth?

 read:

God can't stomach liars; he loves the company of those who keep their word.
(Proverbs 12:22, MSG)

Q: Why do you think God can't stomach liars?

Buy the **truth**, *and do not sell it, also wisdom and instruction and understanding.*
(Proverbs 23:23, NKJV, emphasis added)

Q: Because the writer of this proverb says to purchase truth and not let go of it, what does this say about the importance of truth? Why do you think the writer says "buy"? Isn't truth free?

I am the way, the **truth**, *and the life. No one comes to the Father except through Me.*
(John 14:6, NKJV, emphasis added)

Q: Some have said Jesus is truth with skin on. Recall a story from the New Testament where Jesus spoke the truth to someone. What did He say? How did the person react? (Hint: the woman at the well.)

The Word became flesh and made his dwelling among us. We have seen his glory, the glory of the One and Only, who came from the Father, full of grace and **truth**.
(John 1:14, emphasis added)

Q: Have you ever known someone who was full of grace but didn't tell the truth? How about someone who told the truth but had no grace in telling it? Why do you think Jesus is both grace and truth? Describe someone you know who seems full of grace and truth.

Have you ever known someone who was full of grace but didn't tell the truth? How about someone who told the truth but had no grace in telling it?

Did you know? Jesus said, "I tell you the truth" seventy-eight times in the New Testament.

You belong to your father the devil, and you want to do what he wants. He was a murderer from the beginning and was against the **truth**, *because there is no* **truth** *in him. When he tells a lie, he shows what he is really like, because he is a liar and the father of lies.*

(John 8:44, NCV, emphasis added)

Q: Why do you think the devil is a liar? What does he gain from telling lies? What kind of lies does he tell? Why does he tell them?

Q: What lies do people in your school believe today? What about in your circle of friends?

But everything exposed by the light becomes visible, for it is light that makes everything visible. This is why it is said: 'Wake up, O sleeper, rise from the dead, and Christ will shine on you." *Instead, speaking the* **truth** *in love, we will in all things grow up into him who is the Head, that is, Christ.*

(Ephesians 5:13–14; 4:15, emphasis added)

Q: The apostle Paul equates light with truth in these verses. Why do you think he does that?

Q: How does speaking the truth help us "grow up"?

Q: According to this verse, how do we become more like Jesus?

Talk. ←

So what does all this have to do with you?

Author Anne Lamott wrote: "Risk being unliked. Tell the truth as you understand it."[1]

Q: Why is telling the truth a risk?

Q: Looking back on the sketch you watched, which lies did you most identify with? Why? Which ones did you think might be justified?

KELLIE: It's like we all play some big game of hide-and-seek with each other. And we hurt each other just because we are scared to be ourselves.

Q: When is it hard to be yourself around your friends? your family? When is it easy?

KELLIE: Wouldn't it change things if we were really that honest with each other?

BRIAN: I could never be that honest. People would laugh.

MANDY: They would use whatever I said against me.

JOSH: Because they would still be playing the game, wearing the mask, and then I would be the odd one out.

Q: Why do people sometimes act as though they want to be the odd one out?

Q: Which of these answers best reflects where you are right now?

> *"It's like we all play some big game of hide-and-seek with each other. And we hurt each other just because we are scared to be ourselves."*

---

1 Anne Lamott, *Bird by Bird: Some Instructions on Writing and Life* (New York: Anchor, 1995).

activity: nothin' but the truth.

Write something on a slip of paper that is true about yourself that you're pretty sure no one in your group knows. Put it in a hat or bowl along with everyone else's. Have your leader pull out each truth one by one.

Write everyone's name on a piece of paper. As each truth is read, don't talk or make any expressions. Simply write whose truth you think it is next to his or her name. At the end, reveal your truth. See who guesses the most right.

i love cats

i hate donuts

14

Pray. ←

THE EXAMEN.

What is an Examen? It's a type of prayer and way of relating to God developed by St. Ignatius of Loyola. He came to know Christ after being injured in battle while he recuperated in a hospital. He developed a way to meet with God called the Examen—a type of prayer that divides our prayer time between desolations (feeling sad about stuff) and consolations (feeling happy about stuff). Simply put:

Desolations = Lows

Consolations = Highs

Thinking back over last week, remember the times you were tempted to lie or pretend. Or the times when you decided to hide the real you for some reason.

In terms of truth telling, write down your lows.

Now list your highs, those times you felt truly yourself, when you dared to be honest, even if you upset someone or risked being rejected.

> Examen—a type of prayer that divides our prayer time between desolations (feeling sad about stuff) and consolations (feeling happy about stuff).

_____

_____

_____

_____

As you pray around your group, either silently or out loud, thank God for the highs of your week and pray about your lows. Ask God to help you trust Him when you are tempted to hide or lie. Thank Him for helping you to see when you are afraid of trusting who He made you to be. Ask that He make you more aware of His presence with you throughout the next week.

create.

on Your own Study #I.

ACTIVITY: Two Sides of Yourself.

Supplies needed:

- One playing card (Choose a joker so you won't break up a set.)
- Scissors, glue stick, permanent pens
- Magazines

Sometimes we're situational in the way we live our lives. At home we're one person, at school another, maybe a third entirely different person at church or a party. Today it's time to represent the real *you* to the *you* who may act differently somewhere else.

Choose a place: Home, school, church, party, work, hanging out.

> *Sometimes we're situational in the way we live our lives. At home we're one person, at school another, maybe a third entirely different person at church or a party.*

On one side of the playing card, paste words or images cut from a magazine that represent who you are at that place. (Maybe for church you write the word *good* or *quiet*.)

Once you've covered one side of the card with who you are in that particular place, turn the card over. On this side paste words and images that represent who you truly are. Be yourself. Show yourself.

Q: What place did you choose to write about? Why did you choose that place? Why are you different there?

Q: Is there a particular reason you are afraid to be yourself there?

Q: If you were honestly yourself in the place you chose (being the "me" that is represented on the other side of your card), what would happen? (Cheat: You can't say the earth will implode.)

Think about it:

What you're after is truth from the inside out.
(Psalm 51:6, MSG)

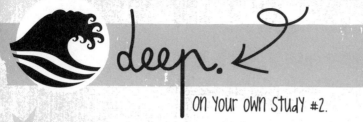

deep.

on your own study #2.

ACTIVITY: Who really knows me?

On your Facebook page (or among a circle of e-mail friends), share two crazy, wacky (but truthful) statements about yourself that very few people know, then write one that is "so not you." See if your friends can quickly identify the one that doesn't represent you. See if you can guess theirs.

Let's go deeper thinking about truth and who you are. Remember the DVD you watched this week where the four characters were forced to tell the truth every time a bell rang?

Q: What "bells" make you tell the truth? Your parents? Getting caught in a lie? Fear of being found out? Worry of what God might think? Fatigue over trying to be everything to everybody? Wondering if it would help?

You cannot fully share the truth about yourself with others unless you know the truth about yourself. It takes courage to understand who you are, how you're wired, why you like what you like and don't like what you don't like. Many of us fear that if we let ourselves "out," others won't like us.

Let's take a ME inventory. As best as you can, based on your life as it is (not as you want it to be), answer the following questions:

Q: Would you rather hibernate in your room or go out to the movies with a group of friends?

Q: What fears do you have that you don't share (snakes, bugs, small spaces)?

Q: When you try to go to sleep at night, what thoughts dominate?

Q: What was your favorite year in school? Why?

Q: What was the worst year? What made it that way?

Q: Have you had a best friend? If so, who was he/she? Are things the same now?

> *You cannot fully share the truth about yourself unless you know the truth about yourself.*

Q: What's your favorite flavor of ice cream?

Q: If you could be amazing at any sport, what would it be?

Q: What is your favorite subject in school? Least favorite?

Q: What food would you like to try? What food will you never eat, no matter what?

Q: Whom do you most admire? Why (ability, personality, character trait) do you admire that person?

Q: What's your favorite song? artist? Do you ever feel the need to adjust your favorites based on what other people like at the time?

Q: If you created a YouTube video of your life this year, what would you title it?

Q: If you could hang out with anyone in the world for one day, who would it be? What would you do with your time? Where in the world would you meet?

Q: What do you want to be when you grow up? What do your parents want you to be?

Q: Who do you want to be when you grow up? What qualities do you want to have as an adult?

Q: What scares you in a movie?

Q: What was your favorite story or book as a kid?

Q: Write five words that you believe describe God.

Think about it:

Your answers to these questions are uniquely yours. No one on the face of this earth will answer them in quite the same way (unless they are cheating off your paper!). You are the only ME there is. Psalm 139:14 (NLT) says, "Thank you for making me so wonderfully complex! Your workmanship is marvelous—how well I know it."

You might say, "Hey, wait a minute. That sounds stuck up. I mean, am I really supposed to feel that way about myself? The people I know that think they're 'all that'—well, nobody really likes them."

There is a difference between trusting ourselves and trusting God with ourselves. Because He *made* us (are you with me?), His perspective is important.

O LORD, you have examined my heart
>   (My heart? Mine? My real heart?)
  and know everything about me.
>   (Everything. Everything? Even that time that I . . . Everything.)
You know when I sit down or stand up.
>   (Or watch TV on the couch? Or run track?)
  You know my thoughts even when I'm far away.
>   (Why doesn't that guy/girl seem interested in me? God, are You really real?)
You see me when I travel
>   (Heading to an out-of-town football game.)
  and when I rest at home.
>   (Please make four hours of sleep count like eight!)
  You know everything I do.
>   (Um, there's that everything word again.)
You know what I am going to say
>   (Why don't I?)
  even before I say it, LORD.
>   (Couldn't You stop me every once in a while?)
You go before me and follow me.
>   (I get it. You are in front of me and behind me—all around me.)
  You place your hand of blessing on my head.
>   (Wait, huh? Blessing on me? Really?)
Such knowledge is too wonderful for me,
>   (I'm not sure this can really be true.)
  too great for me to understand!
>   (It doesn't make sense . . . God's hand of blessing on me while I'm lying on the
>   couch watching TV or wondering if He even exists? Come on, I don't get it.)

I can never escape from your Spirit!
>   (I guess there is nowhere I can go that You aren't there.)
  I can never get away from your presence!
>   (Nowhere that You aren't with me.)
If I go up to heaven, you are there;
>   (I knew that one.)
  if I go down to the grave, you are there.
>   (I'm going to have to take Your word for it, but that's a hard one.)
If I ride the wings of the morning,
>   (Do I have to get up early to do this?)

> "You place your
> hand of blessing
> on my head."
> PSALM 139:5B

if I dwell by the farthest oceans,
> *(I would love to live in California.)*

even there your hand will guide me,
> *(I'm starting to get it—early, late, near, far, high, low.)*

and your strength will support me.
> *(Not only are You there, but You are really there for me when You're there.)*

I could ask the darkness to hide me and the light around me to become night—
> *(I think I've done this before.)*

but even in darkness I cannot hide from you.
> *(Wow, I guess I thought You couldn't see me. Like if I tried not to see You in a dark place, then You wouldn't see me either.)*

To you the night shines as bright as day.
> *(You mean there really is no difference? I don't think I knew this.)*

Darkness and light are the same to you.
> *(As am I, in the dark or the light, because You know ME. The real me. Inside out. Wherever I go, whatever I am doing. You know me. That's just cool.)*

(Psalm 139:1–12, NLT, additions in parentheses)

From these verses, six truths surface:

1. God knows your heart, even the secrets you hide from others.
2. He knows who you are, even if you're unsure.
3. He anticipates what you will say.
4. You cannot outrun His love.
5. He is always nearby.
6. God's hand guides you.

Write a prayer to God based on these six truths. Here's an example based on truth #4:

There are days when I feel You can't love me, Jesus. If only because I can't love myself. But You say I can't outrun Your love, Your presence. Convince me of this on the inside. Give me an understanding of this way down deep where it matters. And when I'm afraid, help me to run to You and not away from You.

Another option:
Go back through the psalm above and write your own words between the (parentheses).

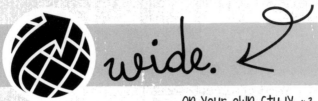

wide.

read:

We have spoken freely to you, Corinthians, and opened wide our hearts to you. We are not withholding our affection from you, but you are withholding yours from us. As a fair exchange—I speak as to my children—open wide your hearts also.

(2 Corinthians 6:11–13)

Paul's example is that of an open life, an authentic heart so others could see the real him. As a result of his openness, he asks the Corinthian church to open their hearts to him. In order to have life-changing relationships with the ones we care about, this kind of exchange must take place. The question is, how do you find the kinds of relationships where people open up their hearts to show you who they really are, and you feel safe enough to be the real you toward them?

In the sketch, Kellie said, "I'm tired of being all phony. Trying so hard to be accepted that I just go around hiding all the time."

Then she said, "Hello, world? My name is Kellie Louise Brown. I'm pretty shy. Sometimes I feel really insecure about the way I look. I like hanging out at church. I think my hair is way too frizzy. I like my parents. I don't like country music. And I've never kissed a guy."

> *How do you find the kinds of relationships where people open up their hearts to show you who they really are, and you feel safe enough to be the real you toward them?*

21

ACTIVITY: Who are You?

Here's a ME-shaped Mad Lib for you to fill out.

Hello, world? My name is ___Madison Blake___ (your name). I'm ___very loud___ (adjective: outgoing, shy, loud, thoughtful). Sometimes I feel really ___embarrassed___ (adjective) about the way I look. I like hanging out at ___T-night___ (noun, name of place). I think my hair is ___ugly___ ___un-perfect hair___ (adjective describing your love-hate relationship with hair). I like ___a boy in my 2nd p.___ (name of someone you really, truly like). I don't like ___pid___ (noun, something you don't like). And I've never ___played lacrosse___ (verb).

In order to open wide your heart, you have to know what's inside you. Here's an exercise you can do now that will help you understand yourself better. (But be forewarned, this is a really fun thing to do with a group of friends.)

List your three favorite movies. (Don't spend a lot of time thinking about them; just list them as they come to mind.)

1. ___Letters to Juliet___
2. ___Curious Case of Benjiamn Button___
3. ___Footlsse___

Now here's the tricky part. Try to find a common thread between all three movies. For instance, if your favorite movies happen to be *Pride and Prejudice*, *Forrest Gump*, and *The Return of the King*, one common thread might be something like people from the outside—outcasts— overcoming huge odds to change the world.

Q: What is a common theme in your movies? In what way does it resonate with a common theme in your life?

Typically this three-movie theme has everything to do with who you are, what you love, and how you see yourself in the world.

Q: Did you find that to be true in your case?

Now take a minute to think through your current friendships. List your top five friends.

1. Kali
2. Sophia
3. Katlin
4. Tesse
5. Kaliegn

Q: Which friends would embrace the real you? The you described in the three-movie exercise?

Q: Which friends would make fun of your movie choices or your theme? Any surprises?

Q: Do you spend more time with friends who accept you or with ones you might have to pretend around? In light of this, does it make sense to make some changes?

Good friends should be like stakes in the ground. When circumstances start to swirl around you, or the world blows this way and that, or you feel that you are in a hurricane of choices and don't know what to do, true friends will be those stakes that help you keep from being blown away. They'll keep you grounded (don't think *punished*; think *secure*) when life gets out of control and threatens to bend you completely over.

Make a choice today to gently open your heart to a friend who seems to know you and accept you. Remember, sometimes your friends can't accept you because they haven't learned yet to accept themselves. So even if you've had a hard time finding a friend like this, know that the One who made you and knows all about you is your friend for life.

When circumstances start to swirl around you, or the world blows this way and that, or you feel that you are in a hurricane of choices and don't know what to do, true friends will be those stakes that help you keep from being blown away.

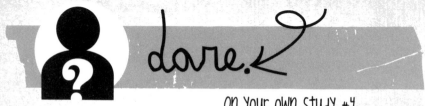

A T-shirt reads, *Be different like everyone else.*

Q: What do you think of that statement?

We all want to be different, and when you think about it, we already are. So why do so many people have to fight to try to prove they are "different" as opposed to just being themselves?

Q: What does it mean to be different, especially when you think about your relationship with Jesus?

Let's look at Jesus for a moment. How was He different?

1. He said things people (particularly religious people) didn't like.
2. He walked away from the crowds that pressed in on him (He was popular!) so He could spend time alone on a mountain to pray.
3. He loved outcasts.
4. He touched lepers.
5. He didn't allow folks to crown Him king.
6. When His disciples were too busy for clamoring kids, Jesus welcomed them on His lap.
7. He spent time with twelve ordinary men, pouring His life into them.

Was He trying to be different?

Let's look at this in terms of your life today:

1. Do you say things people might not like, if you believe what you have to say is important? Why or why not?
2. Do you dare to spend time away from your social life to be quiet enough to hear from God?
3. Do you go out of your way to notice those in your school who may not have friends? Why or why not?
4. Do you take risks with people who differ from you?
5. Do you try to be the center of attention in a crowd? When? Do you try to disappear in a crowd? When?

6. Is your schedule too busy to squeeze in time with your extended family?

7. In what ways, if any right now, do you invest in the lives of others?

The apostle Paul warned about the dangers of living solely for the crowd. He wrote, "Do you think I am trying to make people accept me? No, God is the One I am trying to please. Am I trying to please people? If I still wanted to please people, I would not be a servant of Christ" (Galatians 1:10, NCV).

Q: **What dangers are you aware of in trying to please people instead of God? Has anything ever happened to you because you just tried to "fit in" and go along with others?**

Q: **Are you living in such a way that you perceive God's smile of approval in who you are?**

What dangers are you aware of in trying to please people instead of God? Has anything ever happened to you because you just tried to "fit in" and go along with others?

✶ ACTIVITY: Write some encouragement.

Think of someone you know who truly loves God. Spend ten minutes today writing him/her a card about what you admire. Address the envelope, and send it with a stamp and a prayer.

If you dare:

Think of someone in your school or circle of influence who isn't accepted for their ME. Write his/her name down on an index card, then tape it on your bedroom/bathroom mirror.

Every day this week, talk to God about relating to him/her differently. Form your own words in prayer, but feel free to use some of these as a guide:

Dear Lord, please give me the courage to accept _____ for who he/she really is. Help me to refuse to laugh at _____ even if others do, to refrain from telling any jokes at his/her expense. Instead, give me Your eyes to see _____. Give me Your love to share, and give me Your grace to be kind in every circumstance. I know You'll help me do this because, by Your grace, You have accepted me for who I am. I'm grateful beyond words.

Resources & iTunes List.

Resources.

- **http://revolvetour.com/blog/**
  Did you know Revolve has a blog?

- **http://www.susiemagazine.com/**
  A great place to explore nearly any question or issue you may have.

- Woman at the Well (YouTube video), **http://www.youtube.com/watch?v=Q49BbfgJbto/**
  Slam poetry about the woman at the well. A perfect video that shows how Jesus loves outcasts.

- **http://operationbeautiful.com/**
  This site's tagline is: "Transforming the way you see yourself one post-it note at a time."

- **http://www.thehopeline.com/blogs/dawson/default.aspx/**
  Youth Leader Dawson McAllister's blog. He tells it like it is.

- *Lies Young Women Believe and the Truth That Sets Them Free* by Nancy Leigh DeMoss and Dannah Gresh

 Listen. ←

- "Be Yourself" by Audioslave, *Out of Exile*
- "Our God (Is Greater)" by Chris Tomlin, *Passion: Awakening*
- "From the Inside Out" by Hillsong United, *Mighty to Save*
- "Welcome to My Life" by Simple Plan, *Still Not Getting Any*
- "I surrender" by Aaron Spiro, *Sing*
- "Beautiful Things" by Gungor, *Beautiful Things*
- "Somewhere I Belong" by Linkin Park, *Meteora*
- "Unashamed" by Starfield, *Beauty in the Broken*

kick some grass

BRIEF OUTTAKE: A crazy, funny, serious puppet show extravaganza featuring Sally with a "Jesus Loves Me" T-shirt, Pastor Bill, and Tom, Sally's friend. Together, they try to figure out what it is God wants from them. T-shirt evangelism? Putting on a good show? Authenticity? Memorizing verses for the sake of proving your worth? Sally and Tom struggle with God and each other as they seek to live out their faith honestly.

 watch dvd episode 2.

 GROUP STUDY:

Truth. ←

Go around your circle and share the answer to these questions (and remember to tell the truth!):

Q: What is the most obscure verse you've ever memorized? Why did you choose it?

Q: Whom do you most relate to in the puppet drama? Tom? Sally? Pastor Bill? Why?

Read Maybelle's Story:

I played the game real well. The Christian game. Said all the right words. Hung out with all the right people. Excelled at Bible drills. Earned badges and all. But somewhere in the midst of it, something happened that made the "Christian me" disconnect with the real me. I saw my good friend Charlie get obliterated by my so-called Christian friends. They called him all sorts of names, made fun of him, behind his back *and* to his face, because, well, Charlie says he's gay.

> *I played the game real well. The Christian game. Said all the right words. Hung out with all the right people. Excelled at Bible drills. Earned badges and all.*

I don't really get it, Charlie's gay thing. We've been friends for a long time, and then one day he just says it. I can't go from being his friend one day to rejecting him the next. I just like him the same way I always did. But the ones who stood next to me at the Bible drills and fellowships, who used to be Charlie's friends too, they don't want anything to do with him now. I see his struggle. I see him trying to figure himself out, but how will he include Jesus in the picture if all he hears is how much they hate him? Somebody wrote "abomination" on his locker. I had to look that word up. Wish I hadn't.

I try to tell my Christian friends that they aren't really helping Charlie, but they don't care. I try to tell Charlie that I'm not like them, and neither is Jesus, but he's not sure. And some days I'm not either.

If He really loves us the way I thought, how come those who follow Him don't love certain people at all?

Q: **Have you ever felt like Maybelle?**

Q: **Has there ever been a time in your life when you've felt like an outcast, maybe like Charlie?**

Q: **What does it mean to truly love someone who is different? Is loving someone supposed to make him/her change?**

Word. ←

 read:

You, my brothers, were called to be free. But do not use your freedom to indulge the sinful nature; rather, serve one another in love. The entire law is summed up in a single command: "Love your neighbor as yourself." If you keep on biting and devouring each other, watch out or you will be destroyed by each other.

(Galatians 5:13–15)

Q: Does it seem like Christianity is really about freedom? How?

Q: What does it mean today to serve one another in love? Who, for you, is hard to serve?

Q: What's happened when you've observed your friends "biting and devouring each other"? What do you think people who don't know Christ think when they see the actions of many Christians? Can you give any examples of things you've seen or heard?

read:

You hypocrites! Isaiah was right when he prophesied about you, for he wrote, "These people honor me with their lips, but their hearts are far from me. Their worship is a farce, for they teach man-made ideas as commands from God."

> *What do you think people who don't know Christ think when they see the actions of many Christians?*

Then Jesus called to the crowd to come and hear. "Listen," he said, "and try to understand. It's not what goes into your mouth that defiles you; you are defiled by the words that come out of your mouth."

Then the disciples came to him and asked, "Do you realize you offended the Pharisees by what you just said?"

Jesus replied, "Every plant not planted by my heavenly Father will be uprooted, so ignore them. They are blind guides leading the blind, and if one blind person guides another, they will both fall into a ditch."

29

Then Peter said to Jesus, "Explain to us the parable that says people aren't defiled by what they eat."

"Don't you understand yet?" Jesus asked. "Anything you eat passes through the stomach and then goes into the sewer. But the words you speak come from the heart— that's what defiles you. For from the heart come evil thoughts, murder, adultery, all sexual immorality, theft, lying, and slander. These are what defile you. Eating with unwashed hands will never defile you."

(Matthew 15:7–20, NLT)

Q: **Have you ever met someone who said all the right Christian words but didn't act at all like Jesus? What did that person do that seemed out of character with their beliefs? Did their actions and words confuse you?**

Q: **In the above passage, Jesus is talking about hypocrisy (saying one thing, doing the opposite). Many folks say they don't want anything to do with Christianity because of hypocrisy. What would you say to someone who—as a result of all the hypocrites he/she had seen—refused to believe that God was a loving God?**

Q: **Jesus speaks about the outward and inward here (food going in, words coming out of the heart). He says it's not the outward that messes folks up as much as it is what's inside the heart. What one thing in your heart would you like to be rid of?**

read:

A good person produces good things from the treasury of a good heart, and an evil person produces evil things from the treasury of an evil heart. What you say flows from what is in your heart.

(Luke 6:45, NLT)

You might be saying, "So Jesus was saying that what's in your heart really does come out of your mouth? Uh oh."

Yep.

read:

Going through the motions doesn't please you, a flawless performance is nothing to you. I learned God-worship when my pride was shattered. Heart-shattered lives ready for love don't for a moment escape God's notice.

(Psalm 51:16–17, MSG)

Q: In this drama we see Sally trying to go through the motions, yet she's friendless. And Tom, who struggles outwardly but somehow manages to make friends. And Pastor Bill who tried to be something that he wasn't so as to gain a cool reputation. How does this verse speak to each of the three characters?

 Talk. ←

Activity: verse relay.

Fold a paper airplane, then toss it to someone in your group. Whenever someone throws the airplane to you, share a verse you know or a book of the Bible. You're out if you can't remember either or if you repeat something someone else has already said. Play until you have a winner. (The winner receives . . . the paper airplane!)

Q: Is the person who recited the most verses or books perceived as the most holy person in your group? Why or why not?

In what ways might Christian T-shirts not please God?

Tom said, "Pastor Bill said he thought it was such a great testimony when people share the gospel of Jesus Christ through their T-shirts."

Q: Do you agree? Why or why not? In what ways might Christian T-shirts **not** please God?

The essence of this puppet drama is Tom's wondering, "What does it really take to please God?"

Q: In your opinion, what does it take to please God?

Pastor Bill quietly admitted he had a tattoo. Although there are scriptural references for banning tattoos (specifically, Leviticus 19:28, NCV: "You must not cut your body to show sadness for someone who died or put tattoo marks on yourselves. I am the LORD."), scholars are divided about the issue.

Before reading any further, discuss why you think they might be divided.

What do you think Jesus means when He calls someone a whitewashed tomb?

Some believe the Bible prohibits tattoos. Others see this tattoo passage in the context of Leviticus where God warned His people not to adopt the current pagan practices of the surrounding culture. Tattooing the skin back then was a religious practice, not a form of self-expression, so today's tattoos aren't necessarily a no-no since they're not linked to a pagan ritual. Other scholars who have studied tattoos and Scripture argue that freedom is what the New Testament is about, so tattoos are now permissible in that kind of freedom.

Q: **What advice have you received about tattoos? Do you think they are cool?**

Q: **Is someone more "Jesusy" if they have a "Christian" tattoo?**

Q: **Have you seen a tattoo that made you curious about Jesus or Christianity?**

Q: **What is the coolest tattoo you've seen? Describe it.**

In Matthew 23:27 (NASB), Jesus says to the Pharisees, who were people known for keeping the religious law, "Woe to you, scribes and Pharisees, hypocrites! For you are like whitewashed tombs which on the outside appear beautiful, but inside they are full of dead men's bones and all uncleanness."

Q: **What do you think Jesus means when He calls someone a whitewashed tomb?**

Q: **What is the difference between a tomb and one that has been whitewashed?**

Pray. ←——————————————————————

(Note to leader: **This takes a little bit of preparation. Download the spiritual pathway inventory at http://common.northpoint.org/sacredpathway.html. Be sure to make enough copies for everyone in your group.**)

One of the best ways to make sure our insides match our outsides is to spend time with God in meaningful ways, like prayer. At its heart, prayer is just spending time connecting with God.

Did you know there are many different ways to connect with God? In fact, He has created unique paths so our ME can connect with Him on a multitude of levels. While some connect with Him best when surrounded by great friends, others like to dig deeper into the Bible and study for all it's worth. Others find themselves closest to God when they're singing worship songs. Some of you may feel God's presence when you serve someone less fortunate than yourself. Others need complete solitude and silence to hear from God. Others feel fully alive spiritually when they serve Him through a cause they're passionate about. And others understand and experience God's presence best when surrounded by the beauty of His creation.

> *Did you know there are many different ways to connect with God? In fact, He has created unique paths so our ME can connect with Him on a multitude of levels.*

Which are you? Take the inventory your leader has provided (or go to the Web site mentioned above to download your own) to find out. It may be that you've been trying to connect with God in a way that doesn't really fit you. The purpose of this inventory is to free you up to enjoy God in the unique ways He made you to enjoy Him!

Q: After discovering your spiritual pathway, share with the group one way you'll connect with God this week through that pathway.

Finish your time together by praying for the person on your left, that he/she would find the time to connect with God in a new way this week.

create.

on your own study #1.

A cookie is only as good as its ingredients, right? If you substitute artificial vanilla for real vanilla and use egg substitutes in place of eggs, you'll come out with a different sort of cookie. It may look like a regular cookie, but it will probably taste artificial.

In a similar way, a heart full of real ingredients—no artificial substitutions of love—produces a real life. The ingredients, or what's inside, make for a richer, more authentic life on the outside.

read:

"A tree is identified by its fruit. If a tree is good, its fruit will be good. If a tree is bad, its fruit will be bad. You brood of snakes! How could evil men like you speak what is good and right? For whatever is in your heart determines what you say. A good person produces good things from the treasury of a good heart, and an evil person produces evil things from the treasury of an evil heart."

(Matthew 12:33–35, NLT)

Activity: Take heart.

Today we're going to make "real" heart cookies. The physical ingredients simply serve as a symbol of great, "real" ingredients creating a delicious cookie. Here's the recipe:

A heart full of real ingredients—no artificial substitutions of love—produces a real life.

Preheat oven to 325°.

1 cup melted butter (no margarine or shortening)
3/4 cup brown sugar
1/2 cup white sugar
1 tsp. real vanilla
2 eggs

In a bowl, combine above ingredients together. With a mixer, beat for one minute until combined.

In separate mixing bowl, stir together:

1/4 tsp. salt
1 tsp. baking soda
3 cups all-purpose flour

Once combined, add dry ingredients to the wet ingredients. Add:

1 1/2 cups semi-sweet chocolate chips

Mix 1 minute. Spray a cookie sheet with cooking spray, then drop tablespoonfuls onto the sheet, 12 cookies per sheet. Bake for 10 minutes. Remove from sheet, then cool on a rack.

Now that you've made cookies from "real" ingredients—no boxes here—share them! Think of someone who is a "real" example, producing the good fruit that Jesus refers to in the passage above. Place several of your cookies on a paper plate, cover with plastic wrap, and present them to him/her "just because."

on your own study #2.

When Tom the puppet got fed up with Sally, he blurted, "I'm sick of all this superficial spiritual crap of winning gold stars and eating fishy crackers. Is this what God really wants from us? Isn't there more? This, this . . . T-shirt is why Jesus died on the cross?"

Q: Do you remember what Sally said in response?

She said, "You said *crap*."

She concentrated more on Tom's bad word than she did on the substance of his honest questions. She heard one thing only, neglecting to understand Tom's real heart.

read:

Now one of the Pharisees invited Jesus to have dinner with him, so he went to the Pharisee's house and reclined at the table. When a woman who had lived a sinful life in that town learned that Jesus was eating at the Pharisee's house, she brought an alabaster jar of perfume, and as she stood behind him at his feet weeping, she began to wet his feet with her tears. Then she wiped them with her hair, kissed them and poured perfume on them.

When the Pharisee who had invited him saw this, he said to himself, "If this man were a prophet, he would know who is touching him and what kind of woman she is—that she is a sinner."

> "Is this what God really wants from us? Isn't there more? This, this . . . T-shirt is why Jesus died on the cross?"

Jesus answered him, "Simon, I have something to tell you."

"Tell me, teacher," he said.

"Two men owed money to a certain moneylender. One owed him five hundred denarii, and the other fifty. Neither of them had the money to pay him back, so he canceled the debts of both. Now which of them will love him more?"

Simon replied, "I suppose the one who had the bigger debt canceled."

"You have judged correctly," Jesus said.

Then he turned toward the woman and said to Simon, "Do you see this woman? I came into your house. You did not give me any water for my feet, but she wet my feet with her tears and wiped them with her hair. You did not give me a kiss, but this woman, from the time I entered, has not stopped kissing my feet. You did not put oil on my head, but she has poured perfume on my feet. Therefore, I tell you, her many sins have been forgiven—for she loved much. But he who has been forgiven little loves little."

Then Jesus said to her, "Your sins are forgiven."

The other guests began to say among themselves, "Who is this who even forgives sins?"

Jesus said to the woman, "Your faith has saved you; go in peace."

(Luke 7:36–50)

> **"He who has been forgiven little loves little."**
> LUKE 7:47B

Q: **In the eyes of society, who was more religious, the Pharisees or the sinful woman? What about in God's eyes? What about in your eyes? What do we base these judgments on? What does Jesus base them on?**

Q: **Why did Jesus praise the woman? What was His focus? What was Simon's focus?**

Consider that what she gave him cost her dearly. One denarius equaled one day's wage. Imagine working five hundred days straight (a year and a half) at a job, then taking all the money you had earned, buying a car, then presenting it to a friend who needed one. That is similar to how extravagant her gift was.

Q: **Have you ever seen anyone give a gift like that?**

Jesus looked past the outside to the inside, and saw her heart. He made the following statement to Simon: "He who has been forgiven little loves little" (Luke 7:47b).

Q: What do you think that means?

Q: How much do you think Simon thought he'd been forgiven? What had he spent?

Q: In what ways does it cost you to follow Jesus today (time, reputation, finances)? How have you had to sacrifice for what you believe?

There is a huge difference in the story between the woman who appeared sinful and the Pharisees who appeared holy.

Q: What is the difference?

Q: Who do you think you are closest to in this story? Are you the sinful woman giving extravagantly to Jesus? Are you like Simon, wondering why Jesus would let a sinful woman wash His feet? What character are you most like in Kick Some Grass? What similarities, if any, do you see between the two stories?

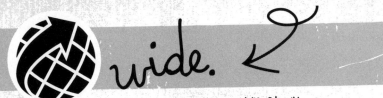

wide.

engagement and purity.

Toward the end of the drama you watched this week, Sally said, "I look at all the friends you have [Tom] and the way people look up to you and they don't to me and you don't seem to try as hard as I do. And I think that instead of witnessing with my T-shirts, I've been driving people away."

Sally put into words an honest struggle.

Q: When is it okay to be good friends with people who broadly differ from our beliefs, and when should we keep ourselves pure?

Aren't we supposed to be set apart, different? And yet, when Jesus walked the earth, every sort of person—with the exception of the religious elite—clamored for His attention. They all wanted to spend time with Him. Why?

Q: How do we connect with all kinds of people with all kinds of problems, yet stay pure?

> *When is it okay to be good friends with people who broadly differ from our beliefs, and when should we keep ourselves pure?*

read:

Religion that God the Father accepts as pure and without fault is this: caring for orphans or widows who need help, and keeping yourself free from the world's evil influence.

(James 1:27, NCV)

Notice how this verse addresses engagement and purity. James said to look after those in need. We're to dirty our hands with the needs of others. And yet, we're to stay pure—to not let the world mold us into its way of thinking or doing things.

read:

Don't copy the behavior and customs of this world, but let God transform you into a new person by changing the way you think. Then you will learn to know God's will for you, which is good and pleasing and perfect.

(Romans 12:2, NLT)

According to this verse, it's possible to hang in the real, gritty world, and yet not let it influence us. We can't go out of the world, hiding behind Christian T-shirts, fearful of interacting with others who are hurting. If we hide, we can't be lights that shine.

read:

In Genesis 12:8, we see Abram (before God renamed him Abraham) pitching his tent in a curious place. Or is it?

From there [Abram] went on toward the hills east of Bethel and pitched his tent, with Bethel on the west and Ai on the east. There he built an altar to the LORD.

What's the big deal about the location of his tent? Oswald Chambers wrote, "Bethel is the symbol of communion with God; Ai is the symbol of the world. Abraham pitched his tent between the two."[1]

> *Oswald Chambers wrote, "Bethel is the symbol of communion with God; Ai is the symbol of the world. Abraham pitched his tent between the two."*

Perhaps that can be a model for us as well as we try to be in the world but live differently from the way the world lives.

Q: **In what ways can you pitch your tent between the world and God? List five ways you can engage with God this week. List five things you can do to rub shoulders with the needs of the world.**

---

1 Oswald Chambers, *My Utmost for His Highest* (Westwood, NJ: Barbour and Company, Inc., 1935), 6.

dare.

BE YOU. BE ONLY YOU.

In the drama, Pastor Bill told Tom, "I didn't listen to the questions inside of me—I just tried to fake it. I was trying too hard to be something for God that He wasn't asking me to be. God didn't want me to be a superstar; He just wanted me to be myself—questions and all."

Many of us freak out about the questions that lurk beneath. We wonder why we're asking hard questions like "Why is there evil in the world?" or "Are there many ways to heaven or just one?" So we tend to stuff our questions deep down inside us, not talk about them, and hope they'll be answered someday, or we decide we don't really need to know the answers after all.

We forget that God sees us and knows every question we push down. Did you know God is big enough to shoulder your questions?

> "I didn't listen to the questions inside of me—I just tried to fake it."

Job was a man in the Old Testament who lost everything—his children, his livestock, his health. At first he didn't question God. He tried to praise Him, even when his wife told him to curse God and beg for death. But eventually as his pain and suffering worsened, he starting asking a few questions. And then a lot of questions. Hard questions. He vented. He gave full wind to his anger. One could say he let God have it. (See Job 26–31.)

Did God run away? Did He worry and wring His hands? Did He hide and hope Job would stop yelling? No. He listened. He absorbed the questions. Then God let loose a few hundred questions of His own. (See Job 38–41.) Questions about creating oceans, placing the sun in the sky, and naming millions of stars. Questions Job could never, given a million years, answer.

> God didn't even answer all of Job's questions. But instead of getting answers, Job got God Himself. That's a pretty good answer.

Here's the thing: relationships can't happen if one person clams up. Death comes to a marriage when one spouse refuses to talk to the other. It's the same in your relationship with God. Job engaged. He raged. He vented his questions. He expressed his feelings and disappointment.

Then God answered.

They had a conversation.

Don't miss what happens at the end of the story. Job—tired, stripped, and as real as he can be—found more of God than he could have imagined. A *real* God, not a God of "Give me what I want and I'll worship You." A really *big* God. Of whom he said, "I know that you can do all things and that no plan of yours can be ruined. . . . My ears had heard of you before, but now my eyes have seen you" (Job 42:2, 5, NCV).

Before all the tragedy, before all the questioning, Job had a hearing relationship with God. He heard from God. He heard of God. But after giving full vent to his questions, Job was able to *see* God. He went from hearing to seeing and experiencing.

And guess what? God didn't even answer all of Job's questions. But instead of getting answers, Job got God Himself. That's a pretty good answer.

Maybe you struggle with your questions. Maybe you worry that God won't like them. But consider this: your questions could be the very road God walks you down to see more of Him in your life. He is not afraid of your questions, and neither should you be. The greater danger is in not asking them.

ACTIVITY: Go ahead, ask Him.

In a quiet place with a notebook or journal in hand, jot down any questions you might have for God. Don't worry about resolving them or prettying them up. Write them raw, undecorated. Questions like:

Why are my parents getting a divorce?

Why don't I seem to fit in at school?

Why is there so much pain in the world?

Now let's ask God to show Himself through our questions.

Father, would You please let me know that I'm not alone in my questions? Would You give me something better than an answer, like Your presence? Sometimes I wonder if You hear me and I'm trusting that You do, even if You can't tell me why I'm going through what I'm going through. I pray that I would see Your hand moving in my life and that I will trust that Your heart is full of love.

Resources & iTunes List.

Resources.

- *Living with Questions* by Dale Fincher
- "God Is Not a White Man" by Gungor (YouTube video),
  http://www.youtube.com/watch?v=-WybvhRu9KU/
  This video shows the extent of God's love for everyone.

- *Finding Out Who You Really Are*, By Design Series, by Melody Carlson
- *To Save a Life* (movie)

 Listen. ⟵ —————————————————————

- "Deciphering Me" by Brooke Fraser, *Albertine*
- "The Scientist" by Coldplay, *A Rush of Blood to the Head*
- "With Arms Wide Open" by Creed, *Human Clay*
- "Deliver Me" by The David Crowder Band, *Illuminate*
- "Who Am I" by Casting Crowns, *Casting Crowns*
- "Keep Quiet" by Barlow Girl, *How Can We Be Silent?*

masks

BRIEF OUTTAKE: Natalie and Jacki seem to like being themselves and feel comfortable in who they are. Then, "the crowd" begins to influence them and a boy comes along and ridicules their choices. Natalie and Jacki begin to wear masks in order to fit in, but both of them discover the high cost of pretending to be something they're not.

watch dvd episode 3.

GROUP STUDY:

 Truth. ←

Go around your circle and share the answer to these questions (and remember to tell the truth!):

Q: When have you told a little white lie to fit in? How did you feel afterward?

Q: Who in your life knows the real you and loves you anyway?

Q: Natalie said, "I used to have a really clear picture of who I was. I mean, if you asked me if I liked something, I knew, and I just said so, straight out." How old were you when you felt you had a clear picture of yourself? What happened in your life when things started to blur?

Read Amber's Story:

I was the girl who always said having an exclusive boyfriend is stupid. I mean, I've seen my friends run off with a guy, then totally neglect every other friendship. I thought it was crazy to spend all your time with a guy, especially one you didn't know all that well.

So when Seth asked me out, I reluctantly said yes. He was the first guy I ever knew who had just the right words to say. I found myself thinking about him all the time. He had these opinions about things I'd never even thought about before. He really liked affection, which meant we had to kiss, hold hands, and other stuff.

I wasn't sure that I wanted to do some of that other stuff. But in the "moment" I was afraid if I didn't that I would lose Seth. All of a sudden he seemed like the world to me. My friends started to make fun of me and roll their eyes because I spent so much time with him. They even said they didn't know me anymore.

I wasn't sure I knew me anymore either. I guess I started trying to become who I thought Seth wanted me to be. Someone I'd never wanted to be, but was now becoming for him.

> *"I used to have a really clear picture of who I was. I mean, if you asked me if I liked something, I knew, and I just said so, straight out."*

One evening his parents were out and we hung out at his house. We were kissing and he was pushing me further than I wanted to go. He said, "You like what I'm doing, right?" And for a moment I couldn't speak, I was so afraid to tell him the truth, to let him see the real me. But the words came up from some place really deep inside: "No, I don't."

I cried all the way home. Lots of heaving in and out. But you know what? It felt good, in a way. At least it was me doing all that crying, not some pretend girl.

Word. ←

read:

Then seizing him [Jesus], they led him away and took him into the house of the high priest. Peter followed at a distance. But when they had kindled a fire in the middle of the courtyard and had sat down together, Peter sat down with them. A servant girl saw him seated there in the firelight. She looked closely at him and said, "This man was with him."

But he denied it. "Woman, I don't know him," he said.

A little later someone else saw him and said, "You also are one of them."

"Man, I am not!" Peter replied.

About an hour later another asserted, "Certainly this fellow was with him, for he is a Galilean."

Peter replied, "Man, I don't know what you're talking about!" Just as he was speaking, the rooster crowed. The Lord turned and looked straight at Peter. Then Peter remembered the word the Lord had spoken to him: "Before the rooster crows today, you will disown me three times." And he went outside and wept bitterly.

(Luke 22:54–62)

Q: How does this story relate to masks?

Q: Why do you think Peter denied knowing Jesus?

Q: Why do you think Peter was more concerned with a servant girl's and two strangers' opinions than Jesus'?

Q: Has there ever been a time in your life that you were afraid to be known as a Jesus-follower? What happened?

Q: Speculate. What do you think would've happened if Peter had not denied Jesus?

Q: Speculate again. The passage says Peter followed Jesus at a distance. Do you think your own mask wearing—if you wear one—has to do with the distance between you and Jesus?

Q: How could being close to Jesus help you unmask?

Talk. ←——————————————————————

Read this poem together. Everyone take a stanza, and read it in your circle, one after the other. We've numbered each stanza for the discussion later.

The mask I wear
Author unknown

1.

Don't be fooled by me.
Don't be fooled by the face I wear
for I wear a mask. I wear a thousand
    masks
masks that I'm afraid to take off
and none of them are me.
That's fine.

2.

Pretending is an art that's second nature
    with me
But don't be fooled; don't be fooled.

3.

I give you the impression that I'm secure
That all is sunny and unruffled with me
within as well as without,
that confidence is my name
and coolness my game,
that the water's calm
and I'm in command,
and that I need no one.

4.

But don't believe me. Please!
My surface may be smooth but my surface
    is my mask,
My ever-varying and ever-concealing
    mask.

5.

Beneath lies no smugness, no
    complacence.
Beneath dwells the real me in confusion,
    in fear, in aloneness.
But I hide this.
I don't want anybody to know it.
I panic at the thought of my weaknesses
and fear exposing them.

6.

That's why I frantically create my masks
    to hide behind.
They're nonchalant, sophisticated facades
    to help me pretend,
To shield me from the glance that knows.
But such a glance is precisely my
    salvation,
my only salvation,
and I know it.

7.

That is, if it's followed by acceptance,
and if it's followed by love.
It's the only thing that can liberate me
    from myself
from my own self-built prison walls.

8.

I dislike hiding, honestly
I dislike the superficial game I'm playing,
the superficial phony game.

9.

I'd really like to be genuine and me.
But I need your help, your hand to hold
Even though my masks would tell you
    otherwise
That glance from you is the only thing
    that assures me
of what I can't assure myself,
that I'm really worth something.

10.

But I don't tell you this.
I don't dare.
I'm afraid to.
I'm afraid you'll think less of me, that
    you'll laugh
and your laugh would kill me.

11.

I'm afraid that deep-down I'm nothing,
    that I'm just no good
and you will see this and reject me.

12.

So I play my game, my desperate,
    pretending game
With a facade of assurance without
And a trembling child within.

13.

So begins the parade of masks,
The glittering but empty parade of masks,
and my life becomes a front.

14.

I idly chatter to you in suave tones of
    surface talk.
I tell you everything that's nothing
and nothing of what's everything,
of what's crying within me.

15.

So when I'm going through my routine
do not be fooled by what I'm saying
Please listen carefully and try to hear
what I'm not saying
Hear what I'd like to say
but what I cannot say.

16.

It will not be easy for you,
long felt inadequacies make my defenses
    strong.
The nearer you approach me
the blinder I may strike back.

17.

Despite what books say of men, I am
    irrational;
I fight against the very thing that I cry out
    for.

18.

You wonder who I am
you shouldn't
for I am everyman
and everywoman
who wears a mask.
Don't be fooled by me.
At least not by the face I wear.

Q: Since everyone had a chance to read a stanza or two, briefly summarize your stanzas. What was the author saying, exactly?

Q: Stanza 3 talks about someone who appears in control, calm even. But he/she says it's a facade. How does insecurity tie in with wearing a mask?

Q: Would your friends say you are insecure? Do you agree?

Q: What does it mean to be secure in who you are?

Q: What do you think the author of this poem is most afraid of?

Q: In stanza 7, the author says love and acceptance are key to taking off the mask. Do you agree? Describe a time in your recent past when you experienced someone's love and acceptance.

Q: When have you experienced God's love and acceptance in the past three months?

Q: The author of the poem deeply fears rejection. Why do we all fear rejection so much? Is it a real fear?

Q: Have you met someone before who initially appeared tough on the outside, but after beginning to trust you, let down his guard? What happened? Why do you think your friend trusted you?

Q: The author wrote, "I fight against the very thing that I cry out for." Have you ever done this? When? Why?

 Pray. ⟵ ──────────────────────────

Choose two stanzas from the poem above: one that represents your struggle today and one that represents a struggle of a friend, acquaintance, or family member. Pray for yourself, then pray for the other person. (Don't mention his/her name.)

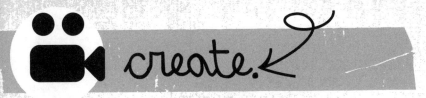

create.

read:

The LORD does not look at the things man looks at. Man looks at the outward appearance, but the LORD looks at the heart. (1 Samuel 16:7)

⭐ ACTiViTY: Mardi Gras mask.

Create a Mardi Gras mask. Here's a place you can print a blank one:
http://familycrafts.about.com/od/makingmasks/ss/EyeMaskTemplate.htm.

On one side of the mask, write words that describe how others see you. Be creative. Add glitter, magazine pictures, vinyl letters.

On the other side of the mask, write how God sees you.

Consider these truths as you write:

1. You are God's child (son, daughter) (John 1:12).
2. You are brand, spanking new (2 Corinthians 5:17)!
3. You are dearly loved, enough to have Jesus die for you (John 3:16).
4. You are unique and known by God (Psalm 139).
5. God delights in your way (Psalm 37:23).
6. God cares about what concerns you (Psalm 138:7).
7. You are forgiven (Ephesians 1:7).
8. You are God's. He made you (Isaiah 43:1).
9. You are not condemned/judged (Romans 8:1).
10. God has reserved a place in heaven for you (1 Peter 1:4).

What you do with your mask is up to you. A few ideas:

1. Hang it in a place you can see it (a mirror, near your computer, etc.).
2. Place it in your Bible.
3. Tuck it in the pages of your journal.

Can you Impress — Less?

BY TODD M. CLEMENTS, M.D.

Many well-meaning teenagers (with likeable personalities) try to impress others as their main mode of operation in pursuing friends and popularity. They think:

- *If my clothes "wow" them, they'll like me.*
- *If I can get more guys interested in me, people will like me.*
- *If I've been more places, done more things, know the right people, make them think my parents are richer, look like I'm smarter, people will like me more.*

Trying to "impress" everyone around you takes massive amounts of time and energy that could be better spent on making real and lasting friendships based on the truth. If you want to make true friendships, work on your listening skills. When you talk to others—instead of thinking about what you're getting ready to say—work at truly listening to what they're saying, and then ask them questions about themselves.

In his book *How to Win Friends and Influence People*, Dale Carnegie says that we can gain more friends in two weeks by becoming interested in other people than we can in two years by trying to get other people interested in us. Give his method a try. I think you might be impressed!

Dr. Todd Clements *is a board-certified psychiatrist and is the medical director of the Clements Clinic in Plano, Texas.*

deep.

read:

And we, who with unveiled faces all reflect the Lord's glory, are being transformed into his likeness with ever-increasing glory, which comes from the Lord, who is the Spirit.

(2 Corinthians 3:18)

Imagine what it would be like to be yourself, completely unmasked, trusting that you are deeply loved by God. This verse describes God's "unveiling" process. A process that will make us each more real. More Jesus-like. More free.

Even though this verse is true, many of us are still afraid. We put on a mask because we want to hide—from our parents, our friends, and even God.

Let's dig a little deeper and look at the very first folks who hid in the Bible.

> **Imagine what it would be like to be yourself, completely unmasked, trusting that you are deeply loved by God.**

read:

Now the serpent was more crafty than any of the wild animals the LORD God had made. He said to the woman, "Did God really say, 'You must not eat from any tree in the garden'?"

The woman said to the serpent, "We may eat fruit from the trees in the garden, but God did say, 'You must not eat fruit from the tree that is in the middle of the garden, and you must not touch it, or you will die.'"

"You will not surely die," the serpent said to the woman. "For God knows that when you eat of it your eyes will be opened, and you will be like God, knowing good and evil."

When the woman saw that the fruit of the tree was good for food and pleasing to the eye, and also desirable for gaining wisdom, she took some and ate it. She also gave some to her husband, who was with her, and he ate it. Then the eyes of both of them were opened, and they realized they were naked; so they sewed fig leaves together and made coverings for themselves.

Then the man and his wife heard the sound of the LORD God as he was walking in the garden in the cool of the day, and they hid from the LORD God among the trees of the garden. But the LORD God called to the man, "Where are you?"

He answered, "I heard you in the garden, and I was afraid because I was naked; so I hid."

And he said, "Who told you that you were naked? Have you eaten from the tree that I commanded you not to eat from?"

The man said, "The woman you put here with me—she gave me some fruit from the tree, and I ate it."

Then the LORD God said to the woman, "What is this you have done?"

The woman said, "The serpent deceived me, and I ate."

(Genesis 3:1–13)

> **Before Adam and Eve sinned, they were naked, completely themselves. . . .**
> **They wore no masks. Nothing existed between them, each other, their God, and their world.**

Consider that before Adam and Eve sinned, they were naked, completely themselves. Not only did they live freely before each other, but they didn't mind living clothing-less when God meandered through the garden of Eden. They wore no masks. Nothing existed between them, each other, their God, and their world.

As Eve took the fruit, then gave it to Adam, shame entered the picture in an ugly rush. Suddenly, they looked at themselves, the same people they'd always been, and were afraid of what they saw. They felt the need to cover up, to hide.

Adam and Eve were the first mask wearers! Theirs looked like fig leaves sewn crudely together. Ours are more sophisticated, but the result is the same: hiding who we really are from one another and God. Living in the fear of being found out. Worrying about being exposed.

Q: List words that described Eden prior to Genesis 3. (Read Genesis 1–2 to gain perspective.)

Q: Now reread the first part of chapter 3. What words describe Eden and the state of Adam, Eve, and God after the Fall?

Did you realize that Jesus came to set things back in place?

read:

For since death came through a man, the resurrection of the dead comes also through a man. For as in Adam all die, so in Christ all will be made alive.

(1 Corinthians 15:21–22)

What was beautiful and whole about Eden before Adam and Eve sinned, Christ will restore. Where there were masks and hiding and fear, Jesus brings freedom, reality, and confidence. Because of Jesus and His resurrection (He conquered death, something Adam and Eve could not), we are made alive. Fully alive. Fully free. Able to be ourselves without masks or lies or pretending.

Take a moment to write out a prayer of thanks in your journal. Look over your list of how Eden was prior to the sin of man. Ask God to restore that kind of wholeness to your life. Look at the words you wrote about Adam and Eve after their sin. Ask God, in writing, to free you from your own tendencies to hide and scheme and self-protect.

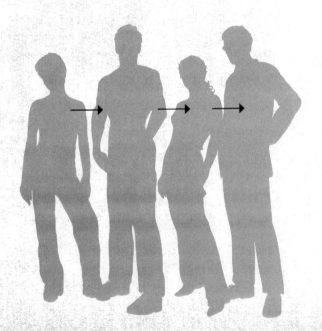

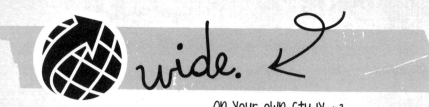

wide.

people usually wear masks out of fear.

We're afraid of being found out. We fear rejection. We worry we won't be loved, accepted, or understood. We don't want to be left out for being different. We would rather pretend and be "in" than be honest and be "out." We fear that if we are truly ourselves, mask-less, our circle of friends won't like us.

It's time to widen our concept of God's love. Why? Because only God's unfailing, unconditional, uncompromising love can settle us from the inside out. By putting your weight down on His acceptance, you'll trade insecurity for security, fear for confidence.

So how wide is God's love? **God's love is deeper than you can imagine**.

read:

And I pray that you, being rooted and established in love, may have power, together with all the saints, to grasp how wide and long and high and deep is the love of Christ, and to know this love that surpasses knowledge—that you may be filled to the measure of all the fullness of God.

(Ephesians 3:17b–19)

We don't want to be left out for being different. We would rather pretend and be "in" than be honest and be "out." We fear that if we are truly ourselves, mask-less, our circle of friends won't like us.

While reading these next verses, substitute *God* for the word *love*. Remember 1 John 4:16 says, "God is love" (NKJV). Reading the verses this way will give you a wider perspective of God's patient love.

Love [God] is patient, love [God] is kind. It [God] does not envy, it [God] does not boast, it [God] is not proud. It [God] is not rude, it [God] is not self-seeking, it [God] is not easily angered, it [God] keeps no record of wrongs. Love [God] does not delight in evil but rejoices with the truth. It [God] always protects, always trusts, always hopes, always perseveres. Love [God] never fails.

(1 Corinthians 13:4–8a)

Q: Have you ever known a love like this? In what ways can you imagine your life would change if you trusted a love like this?

Pop-up news flash: You don't have to have it all together for God to act on your behalf.

> *But God shows his great love for us in this way: Christ died for us while we were still sinners.*
>
> (Romans 5:8, NCV)

> *This is love: not that we loved God, but that he loved us and sent his Son as an atoning sacrifice for our sins.*
>
> (1 John 4:10)

God's love is so great that it drives out fear.

> *There is no fear in love. But perfect love drives out fear, because fear has to do with punishment. The one who fears is not made perfect in love.*
>
> (1 John 4:18)

> *"There is no fear in love. But perfect love drives out fear, because fear has to do with punishment."*
> 1 JOHN 4:18

ACTIVITY: Write it down; put it up.

Write the above verse on a 3" x 5" card and place it on your bathroom mirror. Every day you'll be reminded you don't have to be afraid to be yourself. God's love enables you to live free from fear!

dare.

Jesus saw people on the fringes and dared to elevate them.

In this way, He unmasked all the other people who saw those outcasts and judged them.

read:

A large crowd followed and pressed around him. And a woman was there who had been subject to bleeding for twelve years. She had suffered a great deal under the care of many doctors and had spent all she had, yet instead of getting better she grew worse.

> **Because of her encounter with Jesus, the woman would no longer be an outcast. He healed her "issue" of blood and she was never the same. Those of us who have been freed from our fears and "issues" are never the same either.**

When she heard about Jesus, she came up behind him in the crowd and touched his cloak, because she thought, "If I just touch his clothes, I will be healed." Immediately her bleeding stopped and she felt in her body that she was freed from her suffering.

At once Jesus realized that power had gone out from him. He turned around in the crowd and asked, "Who touched my clothes?"

"You see the people crowding against you," his disciples answered, "and yet you can ask, 'Who touched me?'"

But Jesus kept looking around to see who had done it. Then the woman, knowing what had happened to her, came and fell at his feet and, trembling with fear, told him the whole truth. He said to her, "Daughter, your faith has healed you. Go in peace and be freed from your suffering."

(Mark 5:24b–34)

Q: The woman's bleeding kept her outside of the community. Cast out from her friends and family, she took a huge risk touching Jesus' clothes. And yet He stopped. He turned His focus to just her. How would you feel if Jesus singled you out like that?

Because of her encounter with Jesus, the woman would no longer be an outcast. He healed her "issue" of blood and she was never the same. Those of us who have been freed from our fears and "issues" are never the same either. Here's your dare for the week. Taking this risk will not only bless someone but also help you let go of your own mask.

⭐ ACTIVITY: Frog kissing.

Remember the story about the frog prince waiting for a daring princess to kiss him so he could return to who he was? That's the concept behind frog kissing. Your assignment this week is to find one person who seems to hide, who appears to be on the outskirts of your school or church.

Warning: Do not run up and kiss this person! Instead, think of a creative way to show how important he/she is. Write him a card. Sit with her at lunch. Go out of your way to help someone who seems lost in class to understand the material. Walk around with someone who often walks alone. Invite a new person to your lunch table.

Resources & iTunes List.

Resources.

- Trufaced (YouTube video),
  http://www.youtube.com/watch?v=tIjHKaSyZK4&feature=player_embedded
  From TrueFaced. Great video about wearing masks and being yourself.
- **http://www.truefaced.com/blog/**
  TrueFaced blog.
- "Grey," by BarlowGirl (music video),
  http://www.youtube.com/watch?v=qfHwZzMH_ug/&ob=av2e

 ## Listen. ←

- "Come and Listen," by The David Crowder Band, *A Collision*
- "Enough," by Chris Tomlin, *Not to Us*
- "Hide," by Joy Williams, *Genesis*
- "Wasting Time," by Jack Johnson, *On and On*
- "The Motions," by Matthew West, *Something to Say*

girl of the tombs

BRIEF OUTTAKE: Allison cuts herself. Her therapist asks a lot of questions to get to the bottom of Allison's real pain. A powerful drama that reveals the names we give ourselves and the damage we do by believing lies about our worth.

watch dvd episode 4.

GROUP STUDY:

Truth. ←

Go around your circle and share the answer to these questions (and remember to tell the truth!):

Q: Do you know anyone who has ever cut himself/herself? How did you find out? Have you tried to help him/her?

Q: This drama isn't solely about pulling a blade across skin. It's about hurting ourselves. In what ways do you hurt yourself?

Q: What would your closest friend say is one way you hurt yourself? (This could be negative self-talk, overeating, undereating, isolation, etc.)

Read Kelly's story:

Do you want me to be blatantly honest? I started cutting to be cool. I saw others with marks, asked a few questions, and figured it out for myself. I was tired of being vanilla, if you know what I mean. Tired of the same old same old.

> *"My dad says I'm a drama queen. He may be right. Because I liked the attention I got from my scars."*

My dad says I'm a drama queen. He may be right. Because I liked the attention I got from my scars. I scared my boyfriend. He called my dad, told him to get me somewhere for help. Oh, that made a lot of difference. Dad took me to some shrink, where he sat like a stone, arms folded across his chest, and sighed a lot.

I think he might've cried. Whatever. He's the one who left Mom, forced me to live with him and Patty, and made me move to a new school. Maybe he should cry.

It's not like I'm doing drugs or running around town embarrassing the fam. I get good grades. Really good grades. It's just my little thing. When life feels awkward or scary, I cut myself. A little blood, and it's over. The pain stings, but it feels good.

I look down at my leg or foot and the blood runs down like the tears that don't. Besides, when I bleed, it proves I'm alive. And everyone wants to feel alive, right?

Let's recap the story spoken over the drama.

read:

They came to the other side of the sea, to the country of the Gerasenes. And when Jesus had stepped out of the boat, immediately there met him out of the tombs a man with an unclean spirit. He lived among the tombs. And no one could bind him anymore, not even with a chain, for he had often been bound with shackles and chains, but he wrenched the chains apart, and he broke the shackles in pieces. No one had the strength to subdue him. Night and day among the tombs and on the mountains he was always crying out and cutting himself with stones. And when he saw Jesus from afar, he ran and fell down before him. And crying out with a loud voice, he said, "What have you to do with me, Jesus, Son of the Most High God? I adjure you by God, do not torment me." For he was saying to him, "Come out of the man, you unclean spirit!" And Jesus asked him, "What is your name?" He replied, "My name is Legion, for we are many." And he begged him earnestly not to send them out of the country. Now a great herd of pigs was feeding there on the hillside, and they begged him, saying, "Send us to the pigs; let us enter them." So he gave them permission. And the unclean spirits came out, and entered the pigs, and the herd, numbering about two thousand, rushed down the steep bank into the sea and were drowned in the sea.

The herdsmen fled and told it in the city and in the country. And people came to see what it was that had happened. And they came to Jesus and saw the demon-possessed man, the one who had had the legion, sitting there, clothed and in his right mind, and they were afraid. And those who had seen it described to them what had happened to the demon-possessed man and to the pigs. And they began to beg Jesus to depart from their region. As he was getting into the boat, the man who had been possessed with demons begged him that he might be with him. And he did not permit him but said to him, "Go home to your friends and tell them how much the Lord has done for you, and how he has had mercy on you." And he went away and began to proclaim in the Decapolis how much Jesus had done for him, and everyone marveled.

(Mark 5:1–20, ESV)

"Night and day among the tombs and on the mountains he was always crying out and cutting himself with stones."
MARK 5:5 (ESV)

Q: What would it be like to live in tombs? Why do you think the man chose to live there?

Q: The Scripture says that the demons drove the man to solitary places, places where he was utterly alone. When have you felt most alone? Why do you think we seek to be by ourselves at the times we feel the worst?

Q: The townspeople seemed to be more concerned for the pigs (which represented money to them) than they were for the man. Why do you think that is?

Q: After Jesus delivered the man from the torture he had been enduring, what was the man's response?

Q: What must've it been like for the disciples to witness this strange event?

Q: How is the girl in the drama, Allison, similar to the "demoniac"? How is she different?

 Talk. ←

Q: Many people think cutting (or self-mutilation) is new, even trendy. But if it's in the Bible, how long has it been around? Why do you think this is so?

In the beginning of the sketch, the therapist asked Allison what names she had for herself. She said, "Stupid, maybe. Ugly." The therapist added these words: *sad, hurt, angry, enraged.*

> *The therapist asked Allison what names she had for herself. She said, "Stupid, maybe. Ugly." The therapist added these words: sad, hurt, anger, rage.*

Q: What words describe you today? What words described you three years ago? What words do you want to describe you? (We'll explore this later in study #2.)

The therapist said, "Teenage girls face enormous pressure to split into false selves. They are often faced with the choice to be true to their 'self' and risk abandonment or compromise the 'self' to be more acceptable." For Allison, the choice wasn't happening at school as it does for many girls. The fork in the road between her real self and her false self was at home.

Q: How about you? Where do you find it hardest to be yourself? Home? Church? School? With friends? Why?

The therapist said, "Allison didn't want to kill herself; she cut her feet to keep from killing herself. She didn't want to explode, probably something she saw her dad do regularly. She wanted to keep it all under control. She had to—to survive."

Q: What do you do when you sense your life is slipping out of control? Have you ever noticed a pattern in how you react? What do you do to cope when you feel pain?

Q: Why do you think Allison cut herself?

The therapist said, "I think you would rather feel the pain from cutting than the pain from all you can't understand in your own life. It might even help you make sense of things—which is why you feel relief when it's over. But it doesn't last because you come out and [your father] is still there."

Q: Why do you think Allison felt relief for a short period of time after she cut herself? Why doesn't the relief last?

Q: How does doing something destructive help people understand life? List several things Allison could do besides cutting to try to cope with her angry father.

> *How does doing something destructive help people understand life?*

 Pray.

wallet Prayers.

Give every person in the study a small piece of paper (a little larger than a fortune in a fortune cookie). Instruct them to write the name of a person on their slip of paper, someone they're deeply concerned about, someone who is doing something self-destructive. It can even be their own name.

Once written, have them fold their paper and place it in their wallet safe and out of the way.

Spend thirty seconds per person in the group in silent prayer. (Six people equals three minutes of silence.) Let them fill the silence with their own silent prayers for their wallet friend. End the time by praying out loud, generically praying for every person represented by those slips of paper.

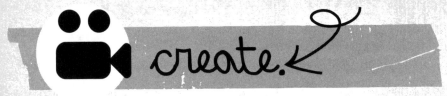

on Your own STudY #1.

One of the most beautiful forms of psalms is the Lament Psalm. Perhaps this is why many people facing troubles and stress and overwhelming circumstances turn to the psalms, particularly the Lament.

The structure of the Lament Psalm is something that helps you move through grief to relief, ending in praise. Here is the structure:

1. A rant to God, maybe a why-is-this-happening-to-me question
2. A description of your current stress or problem
3. A request to God, something like, "Please help me!"
4. God's specific answer to you in the middle of your pain
5. Your words of trust in the God who hears your lament

See if you can pick out the five phases of a Lament Psalm.

read:

How long, O Lord? Will you forget me forever?
　　How long will you hide your face from me?
How long must I wrestle with my thoughts
　　and every day have sorrow in my heart?
　　How long will my enemy triumph over me?
Look on me and answer, O Lord my God.
　　Give light to my eyes, or I will sleep in death;
my enemy will say, "I have overcome him,"
　　and my foes will rejoice when I fall.
But I trust in your unfailing love;
　　my heart rejoices in your salvation.
I will sing to the Lord,
　　for he has been good to me.
　　　　(Psalm 13)

Activity: It's your turn to rant.

Now it's your turn. Write your own Lament Psalm based on the five steps above. Start with a rant. Describe your problem in detail. Ask God to help you figure out your problem, or ask for His presence in the middle of it. Seek God for His answer, then write words that show your trust in Him, even when life hurts.

Many people facing troubles and stress and overwhelming circumstances turn to the psalms, particularly the Lament.

Are You Hurting Yourself?

BY TODD M. CLEMENTS, M.D.

In the last tens years society has become increasingly aware of the issue of self-injury among teenagers. Cutting is often mistakenly termed a suicide attempt or gesture, but in reality it's a way (although an unhealthy way) of coping with overwhelming emotions such as sadness, rage, desperation, and emptiness. Cutting brings an almost immediate feeling of calmness, release of tension, or even a euphoric sense of well-being. Some people report that they feel numb and disconnected from life and when they cut, the pain wakes them up and they feel alive. From a scientific standpoint this makes sense, since in response to physical pain your brain releases a natural chemical called endorphin, which is often referred to as our body's natural pain-killer. Endorphins also calm anxiety, relieve depression, and bring on euphoria.

The problem with getting an endorphin fix from cutting is that endorphins don't stay in your system very long; the painful emotions return, often accompanied by shame and guilt for hurting yourself. Not to mention that open cuts and burns can become infected and leave lifelong scars.

Are You Hurting Yourself? (CONTINUED)

Many cutters plan to stop soon or tell themselves this is the last time, but without creating a plan of action, self-injury can get worse. Cutting is habit forming and the cuts get deeper. So if you have been injuring yourself and would like to stop, here's a good way to get started:

1. Tell someone about it—don't be too embarrassed to ask for help. I recommend seeing a counselor who has experience in dealing with self-injury. It may freak other people out, but a good counselor will know exactly where you're coming from.

2. Learn to identify your triggers—what is it that revs up the urge for you to cut? Perhaps it's an argument with your boyfriend, a bad hair day, or chaos at home? Maybe you're not sure. That's fine. Your counselor can help you gain better insight.

3. Be willing to work on it. This includes figuring out different (and healthier) behaviors you can do when you get the urge to cut. There are other ways to get an endorphin release and change the way you're feeling. Many cutters have found that exercise, journaling, and even talking with friends relieves their urge to cut.

4. Purpose to implement these behaviors into your life—you won't be perfect, especially at first. Finding someone you trust who can hold you accountable will help too.

Dr. Todd Clements *is a board-certified psychiatrist and is the medical director of the Clements Clinic in Plano, Texas.*

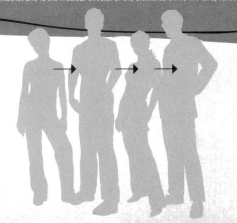

deep.

on Your own Study #2.

In the drama, Allison's therapist said, "Isn't it interesting that the people were more concerned for the pigs than they were for the man? They were appalled and worried over the loss of the commodity. Pigs were the lowest of creatures, the dirtiest of animals, and the people placed more value on them than on this man's life. No wonder he was so tortured."

Q: Have you ever felt second place to things or money? When? How did it/does it make you feel?

Q: Have you ever valued things more than you value people? When?

The therapist said, "When they saw the man clothed and sitting in his right mind, they were afraid. Why then? They were more comfortable with his unclean spirits than with his sanity."

Q: If you have chaos in your life, and you've learned to live with it, chances are, chaos has become your comfort zone. Sometimes it's really hard to move toward health if you've settled for unhealthy (rage, manipulation, abuse) ways of living. In what ways do you prefer staying in the chaos? Name one healthy choice you can make this week.

> *If you have chaos in your life, and you've learned to live with it, chances are chaos has become your comfort zone.*

read:

The LORD will strike Egypt, and then he will bring healing. For the Egyptians will turn to the LORD, and he will listen to their pleas and heal them.

(Isaiah 19:22, NLT)

Sometimes we are hurt by circumstances in our lives that God allows. Your job is not to injure yourself, but to let God use the injury in your life to change you. He has demonstrated that He can use such injuries to actually heal us.

Q: In what ways has God used the painful experiences of your life to bring you to Himself? How has He answered your pleas?

> No matter what you think about yourself or what other names people have called you, you are loved by Jesus. He adores you.

Q: When have you experienced healing from a past trial?

The therapist said, "You feel worthless, angry, ugly, and stupid. But none of those are your names. And your name is not 'cutter' either. Your name is Allison. Your name is 'daughter.' Your name is 'safe.' Your name is 'loved.'"

Q: What are some of the names—positive or negative—that you've given yourself? List them.

Q: What are some positive names others have given you?

Q: What are some negative names others have called you?

Q: Of all the names listed, which ones are the most accurate?

Q: What names does God give you? You might want to choose from the following list:

1. Loved	10. Cherished	19. Prized
2. Healed	11. Valued	20. Pure
3. Affirmed	12. Needed	21. Adored
4. Forgiven	13. A fragrance	22. Washed
5. Set free	14. Hopeful	23. New
6. Radically changed	15. Beloved	24. Renewed
7. Alive	16. Changed	25. Rejuvenated
8. Beautiful	17. Redeemed	
9. Broken, but strong	18. Joyful	

Take those words and text them to yourself. Keep the text as a reminder of who you are. No matter what you think about yourself or what other names people have called you, you are loved by Jesus. He adores you. He holds you when no one else sees your tears. He sees you when you try to destroy yourself. He wants to take away your pain and your brokenness if you will allow Him.

He offered His blood, so you wouldn't have to offer yours.

That is the truth.

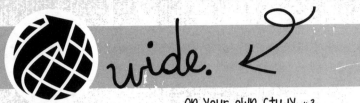

wide.

read this poem:

Come away
And meet the real Me
Not the one you've
Made Me to be
The One
Who took the shame
Untied the knots
With My once-is-enough sacrifice
To set you free
Once-for-all
My voice isn't
What you think it is
But you've made it so
Thinking Me a harsh deity
Like an angry Hindu god
Bent on destroying
Every little sin

Every little piece of you
You forget
That I
Carried it all
Shed My blood
And said It Is Finished
Can you let it be
Finished?
Or will you spend your life
Atoning your Eve-bent ways?
Let it be
Let it lie
Let it go
And let Me peel away the shame
Memory
By
Memory[1]

> *My voice isn't*
> *What you think it is*
> *But you've made it so.*

Q: What stood out to you as you finished this poem?

Q: How does remembering Jesus' willing suffering on your
behalf help you cope with today?

Q: How would the words of this poem help a person who cut herself? Why?

Q: What does it mean that Jesus took the shame of our lives?

---

1 Mary DeMuth, *Thin Places* (Grand Rapids: Zondervan, 2010), 131–32.

read:

Remember, dear brothers and sisters, that few of you were wise in the world's eyes or powerful or wealthy when God called you. Instead, God chose things the world considers foolish in order to shame those who think they are wise. And he chose things that are powerless to shame those who are powerful. God chose things despised by the world, things counted as nothing at all, and used them to bring to nothing what the world considers important. As a result, no one can ever boast in the presence of God.

God has united you with Christ Jesus. For our benefit God made him to be wisdom itself. Christ made us right with God; he made us pure and holy, and he freed us from sin. Therefore, as the Scriptures say, "If you want to boast, boast only about the LORD."

(1 Corinthians 1:26–31, NLT)

> **God actually delights in helping people who are weak. He loves to come alongside those who feel needy to "shame those who are powerful."**

Allison, the girl in the drama you watched, felt helpless to control her situation. She felt lost and scared. She probably felt foolish, powerless, and very needy for love. Yet this verse assures us all that God actually delights in helping people who are weak. He loves to come alongside those who feel needy to "shame those who are powerful."

Why? Because God's strength can't be felt when we're feeling particularly powerful. Think of how much Allison's father ranted and raved. He was not relying on God's strength, but instead using his own. God's strength is a unique kind of strength that only comes out through our weakness. In a strange way, folks like Allison are actually closer to experiencing God's presence because they know their need.

Write a prayer to God, letting Him know where you feel weak today. Ask for His strength. Pray for His power to come in your weakness to help you overcome whatever you're facing. Date the prayer, then fold it into the page next to 1 Corinthians 1:26–31. Maybe you'll rediscover your prayer on a day you'll need it.

Another option:

Go to http://FutureMe.org. There, you can write your prayer (or a letter to yourself) and have it e-mailed to you in the future.

dare.

on your own study #4.

You may have a friend who's going through something like Allison—dealing with deep family pain or past abuse, by self-injury. Or you may have a depressed friend. Or maybe you're in that place. Here are some things to keep in mind as you look after yourself and love your friends.

when people are hurt, they usually react in three ways:

1. Withdraw
2. Get mad
3. Take charge and deal with the problem

The healthiest way to deal with a problem is to find good friends, counselors, or parents and talk through the issue. Pulling away seldom helps. Filling yourself with rage may feel empowering for a moment, but it hurts others.

Here are several healthy ways you can deal with a problem right now:

1. Take some time out, particularly if you have a hectic schedule, and think. Journal your stress.
2. Find a trusted friend and share what's going on.
3. Schedule for yourself (date and time) an activity that brings you joy—hiking, creating art, playing an instrument, taking pictures, calling a close friend, making a meal.
4. Listen to your favorite happy music.
5. Exercise.

Signs of trouble (either for you or a friend):

1. Not sleeping, always tired
2. Pulling away from social things
3. Avoiding friends
4. Only thinking about the issue and nothing more
5. Having surprising outbursts—anger, crying, shouting

The healthiest way to deal with a problem is to find good friends, counselors, or parents and talk through the issue. Pulling away seldom helps.

6. Using drugs or alcohol, prescription medication (not your own)
7. Not eating well, or binge eating
8. Seeing a complete reversal in personality

More Serious Signs (could Signal Suicide):

1. Talking of killing themselves
2. Giving away things they love
3. Writing good-bye letters to friends
4. Saying no one in the world cares for them
5. Believing there is no hope for the future

How to help a friend in a desperate situation:

Don't:

1. Try to shoulder the problem alone.
2. Say platitudes like "Just think happy thoughts."
3. Keep threats or hints of suicide a secret. Find a parent, counselor, or trusted adult to help. You can't solve this problem on your own.

> *Whatever you do, don't do life alone. Don't try to help a friend in deep pain all by yourself. . . . You need a community of others to help you help someone.*

Do:

1. Believe what they tell you.
2. Encourage them to talk to other friends and not isolate themselves.
3. Listen carefully. Ask questions.
4. Think of ways to creatively show you care. (Sending cards, texting, calling, surprising, etc.)
5. Validate how they are feeling.
6. Share your concern.
7. Say you're so glad they're alive.
8. Offer to go with them to a counselor or trusted adult.

Whatever you do, don't do life alone. Don't try to help a friend in deep pain all by yourself. Even a great swimmer is little help to a drowning person without other help. You need a community of others to help you help someone.

Are You Depressed?

BY TODD M. CLEMENTS, M.D.

The latest statistics show that more than one out of ten adolescents struggle with depression. Many adults with depression say it started when they were teenagers.[2] The good news is depression can be successfully treated over 80 percent of the time.[3] The bad news is teenagers often miss out on the opportunity to get help because:

(1) they don't recognize they are depressed;
(2) they feel too ashamed to tell anyone.

Here are some of the most common symptoms of depression:

- Sadness, for most or all of the day
- Appetite changes (less appetite than normal, but occasionally an increase in appetite)
- Feeling excessively guilty—often for things that normally wouldn't bother you
- Lack of desire to hang out with good friends
- Poor concentration or episodes of memory loss
- Feelings of worthlessness
- Thoughts about suicide
- Feeling like life is not worth living—and that your future is bleak
- Problems sleeping (often waking up very early and being unable to go back to sleep)
- Feeling moody, irritable, or having a short fuse

Depression is nothing to be ashamed of. It does not mean you are weak or inferior. In teenagers it can result from conflict with parents, a breakup with a boyfriend or girlfriend, the death of a friend or family member, struggles in school, fluctuation of sex hormones, and general stress. All of these things can create feelings of depression or cause the levels of certain chemicals in your brain to get out of balance.

If you recognized any of the symptoms above in yourself or think you may be struggling with depression, then I urge you to talk with someone about it. Your school counselor or family doctor is a great place to start.

Dr. Todd Clements *is a board-certified psychiatrist and is the medical director of the Clements Clinic in Plano, Texas.*

---

2   James N. Butcher, Susan Mineka, and Jill M. Hooley, *Abnormal Psychology*, 14th ed. (Boston: Allyn & Bacon, 2010), 542.

3   "What Is Depression?" Stanford University School of Medicine Depression Research Clinic, http://med.stanford.edu/depression/depression.html.

Resources & iTunes List.

Resources.

- *Scars That Wound, Scars That Heal* by Jan Kern
- *Self-Injury: When Pain Feels Good* by Edward T. Welch
- *Cut: Mercy for Self-Harm* by Nancy Alcorn

 ## Listen. ←

- "Everything Falls," by Fee, *Hope Rising*
- "Mirror," by BarlowGirl, *BarlowGirl*
- "The Way She Feels," by Between the Trees, *The Story and the Song*
- "Deliver Me," by The David Crowder Band, *Illuminate*
- "How to Save a Life," by The Fray, *How to Save a Life*
- "Cut," by Plumb, *Chaotic Resolve*
- "I'm Not Alright," by Sanctus Real, *The Face of Love*